SUN | MON | TUE | WED | THJ | F

Oli Kids Co.

My 2025
Learning Calendar

Ribbon Star Press

For information regarding written permission, write to:

Ribbon Star Press
2842 Main Street #110
Glastonbury, CT 06033

ISBN 979-8-9894288-0-9
Published by Ribbon Star Press, a division of Next Door Creations, LLC.
Oliver Poons and associated logos are trademarks of Next Door Creations, LLC.

This Book Belongs to:

....

January

- January is the first month of the year, or month number 1.
- The season is winter.
- Two of the special days in January are New Year's Day and Martin Luther King Jr. Day.
- Fill in the boxes with your important information to remember.
- Is your birthday in January? _____
- How many days are in January? ___
- Which month is next month? Turn the page to find out!

_____

JANUARY 2025

SUN	MON	TUE	WED	THU	FRI	SAT
			1 New Year's Day	2	3	4
5	6	7	8	9	10	11
12	13	14	15	16	17	18
19	20 Martin Luther King Jr. Day	21	22	23	24	25
26	27	28	29	30	31	Notes

February

- February is the second month of the year, or month number 2.

- The season is winter.

- Some of the special days in February are: Groundhog Day, Valentine's Day, Presidents Day, and the start of Ramadan.

- Fill in the boxes with your important information to remember.

- Is your birthday in February? ____

- Which month was last month?
  _____

- Which month is next month?
  _____

FEBRUARY 2025

SUN	MON	TUE	WED	THU	FRI	SAT
						1
2 Groundhog Day	3	4	5	6	7	8
9	10	11	12	13	14 Valentine's Day	15
16	17 Presidents Day	18	19	20	21	22
23	24	25	26	27	28 Ramadan Begins	Notes

<u>March</u>

- March is the third month of the year, or month number 3.
- The season is spring.
- One of the special days in March is St. Patrick's Day.
- Fill in the boxes with your important information to remember.
- Is your birthday in March? _____
- Which month was last month? _____
- Which month is next month? _____
- Which day of the week is March 17th? _____

MARCH 2025

SUN	MON	TUE	WED	THU	FRI	SAT
						1
2	3	4	5	6	7	8
9	10	11	12	13	14	15
16	17 St. Patrick's Day	18	19	20	21	22
23 30	24 31	25	26	27	28	29

April

- April is the fourth month of the year, or month number 4.
- The season is spring.
- Some of the special days in April are: April Fools' Day, Passover, Good Friday, Easter, Earth Day, and Arbor Day.
- Fill in the boxes with your important information to remember.
- Is your birthday in April? _____
- Which month was last month?

  _____
- Which month is next month?

  _____
- Say the days of the week: Sunday, Monday, Tuesday, Wednesday, Thursday, Friday, Saturday

APRIL 2025

SUN	MON	TUE	WED	THU	FRI	SAT
		1 April Fools' Day	2	3	4	5
6	7	8	9	10	11	12 Passover Begins
13	14	15	16	17	18 Good Friday	19
20 Easter	21	22 Earth Day	23	24	25 Arbor Day	26
27	28	29	30	Notes		

<u>May</u>

- May is the fifth month of the year, or month number 5.

- The season is spring.

- Some of the special days in May are: Cinco de Mayo, Mother's Day, and Memorial Day.

- Fill in the boxes with your important information to remember.

- Is your birthday in May? _____

- Which month was last month?

  _____

- Which month is next month? Turn the page to find out! _____

- Which day of the week is May 5th?

  _____

- Which day comes after Sunday?

  _____

MAY 2025

SUN	MON	TUE	WED	THU	FRI	SAT
				1	2	3
4	5 Cinco de Mayo	6	7	8	9	10
11 Mother's Day	12	13	14	15	16	17
18	19	20	21	22	23	24
25	26 Memorial Day	27	28	29	30	31

June

- June is the sixth month of the year, or month number 6.

- The season is summer.

- Some of the special days in June are: World Environment Day, Flag Day, Father's Day, and Juneteenth.

- Fill in the boxes with your important information to remember.

- Is your birthday in June? _____

- How many days are in June? _____

- What is the weather like in June? _____

- Which day of the week is June 21st? _____

JUNE 2025

SUN	MON	TUE	WED	THU	FRI	SAT
1	2	3	4	5 World Environment Day	6	7
8	9	10	11	12	13	14 Flag Day
15 Father's Day	16	17	18	19 Juneteenth	20	21
22	23	24	25	26	27	28
29	30	Notes				

<u>July</u>

- July is the seventh month of the year, or month number 7.
- The season is summer.
- One of the special days in July is Independence Day.
- Fill in the boxes with your important information to remember.
- Is your birthday in July? _____
- How many days are in July? _____
- Are there more days in June or July? _____
- Which day of the week comes after Wednesday? _____

JULY 2025

SUN	MON	TUE	WED	THU	FRI	SAT
		1	2	3	4 Independence Day	5
6	7	8	9	10	11	12
13	14	15	16	17	18	19
20	21	22	23	24	25	26
27	28	29	30	31	Notes	

<u>August</u>

- August is the eighth month of the year, or month number 8.
- The season is summer.
- One of the special days in August is Women's Equality Day.
- Fill in the boxes with your important information to remember.
- Is your birthday in August? _____
- Which month has the fewest days? Look through this book to find out.

  _____
- Which days are the two weekend days? Hint: They both start with an 'S'.

  _____

AUGUST 2025

SUN	MON	TUE	WED	THU	FRI	SAT
					1	2
3	4	5	6	7	8	9
10	11	12	13	14	15	16
17	18	19	20	21	22	23
24 / 31	25	26 Women's Equality Day	27	28	29	30

September

- September is the ninth month of the year, or month number 9.
- The season is fall.
- Two of the special days in September are Labor Day and Grandparents Day.
- Fill in the boxes with your important information to remember.
- Is your birthday in September?____
- Which month was last month?

  _____
- Which month is next month? Turn the page to find out. _____
- Which season comes before fall?

  _____

SEPTEMBER 2025

SUN	MON	TUE	WED	THU	FRI	SAT
	1 LABOR DAY Labor Day	2	3	4	5	6
7 Grandparents Day	8	9	10	11	12	13
14	15	16	17	18	19	20
21	22	23	24	25	26	27
28	29	30	Notes			

October

- October is the tenth month of the year, or month number 10.
- The season is fall.
- Two special days in October are Columbus Day and Halloween.
- Fill in the boxes with your important information to remember.
- Is your birthday in October? _____
- What does the weather feel like in fall? _____
- How many days are in October?_____
- Find another month with 31 days.

_____

OCTOBER 2025

SUN	MON	TUE	WED	THU	FRI	SAT
			1	2	3	4
5	6	7	8	9	10	11
12	13 Columbus Day	14	15	16	17	18
19	20	21	22	23	24	25
26	27	28	29	30	31 Halloween	

November

- November is the eleventh month of the year, or month number 11.
- The season is fall.
- Two special days in November are Veterans Day and Thanksgiving.
- Fill in the boxes with your important information to remember.
- Is your birthday in November? _____
- How many days are in November? __
- Which day of the week is November 18th? _____
- How many days are in a week? _____

NOVEMBER 2025

SUN	MON	TUE	WED	THU	FRI	SAT
						1
2	3	4	5	6	7	8
9	10	11 Veterans Day	12	13	14	15
16	17	18	19	20	21	22
23 30	24	25	26	27 Thanksgiving	28	29

December

- December is the twelfth month of the year, or month number 12.

- The season is winter.

- Some of the special days in December are: Christmas, Hanukkah, and New Year's Eve.

- Fill in the boxes with your important information to remember.

- Is your birthday in December? _____

- Say all the days of the week.

- Say all the months of the year. Use this book for help.

- What is your favorite month?

  _____

- Why is this your favorite month?

  _____

DECEMBER 2025

SUN	MON	TUE	WED	THU	FRI	SAT
	1	2	3	4	5	6
7	8	9	10	11	12	13
14	15	16	17	18	19	20
21	22	23	24	25 Christmas Day Hanukkah Begins	26	27
28	29	30	31 New Year's Eve	Notes		

Join us for more fun and learning on OliKidsCo.com!

Ribbon Star Press